John Pawson
Themes and Projects

John Pawson
Themes and Projects

'When the stars are propitious, a foreword is not a subordinate form of salutation, it is a lateral kind of criticism', Jorge Luis Borges said in his mirror-like book of 1975 entitled *Prólogos con un Prólogo de Prólogos*. This book acts as just such a foreword to the work of the architect John Pawson, to his manners, modes, materials and choices of themes in construction: mass, light, structure, ritual, landscape, order, containment, repetition, volume, essence and expression.

These are not merely themes or ideas to be found in his architecture, they are his working materials. And so this book becomes a 'free-standing' foreword to the works that it introduces. In this book the reader will not survey a series of models and dates, a chronology of architecture and an endless sequence of mute plans that no longer speak for themselves or speak only to the architect.

Pawson's simple architecture is built, primarily, with the material called light, in the tradition of Louis Kahn, a material that is combined with or embodies a certain poetry and in which visual effects are metaphors, or rather haiku, simple messages in form and expression but with an intense way of thinking.

His architecture is tranquil, like a night among the dunes of the desert. There is something in Pawson's spaces that comes from the Pre-Romanesque architecture of Asturias, those small churches that at first sight look like palaces and finally seem to be houses into which light enters, or like the pelota courts in the Basque Country, or the prehistoric architecture of Menorca: stone on stone, the simplicity of proportion and restraint. A house built of stone or concrete is really like a tomb. It is almost better to live in a tent: for the Tuareg, the finest sensation of habitation consists in lying beneath the sky and gazing at the stars. In Pawson there is a combination of Calvinist religion and Zen spirit, a mixture of Japanese and Asturian Pre-Romanesque: immaculate spaces, passage walls without skirting or with suspended skirting, and rigid chairs like benches carved out of stone. His houses are like the paintings of another Calvinist in the history of art, another composer of Pre-Byzantine icons, white on white: Malevich.

His interiors are not only diaphanous, they are utterly bare, and the lighting is characteristically indirect. What Pawson does is to bring out the subtlety of large walls. Neutralizing space in terms of the objects that occupied it before in order to let space itself materialize: to let people inhabit it. That is the essence of architecture in the words of Martin Heidegger, 'constructing in order to inhabit, inhabiting in order to think'.

With the use of technology Pawson achieves the dematerialisation of the building, using structures so that the building, the inner space, vanishes visually amidst apparent fragility and transparency, thus achieving a poetics of stillness. Sharply defined architecture, ample spaces, white interiors, a balance of forms and materials – in Pawson's work the boundary between interior and exterior disappears. He manages to make structure and place, light and illumination become one and the same. Sometimes he only transforms the interior space, as in his own home, where, for example, the opening roof in the bathroom creates a new context of use with the possibility of receiving rain an openness to a kind of luxury.

Our automatic thinking about luxury associates it with the concept of privilege, and with money, hence with the inaccessible. It seems as if luxury cannot be democratic or well-distributed like common sense. It has to be something exclusive, with strong sensations and acclamations, with opulence and ostentation. But the notion of luxury, luxuriating in objects and sight, can be different. Luxury is a state of mind, an appetite that one must know how to satisfy and administer like gastronomy, free time or sport. Otherwise, everything becomes a machine, a closed construction, like Olympic athletes. Luxury in architecture is not extravagance, rather it is simplicity.

Pawson has introduced minimalism as luxury, somewhere between Calvinism and luxuriating in simply drinking water, for the aim in life is to achieve excellence. I think it is in *The Seven Lamps of Architecture*, published in 1849, or in the second book of *The Stones of Venice*, which appeared in 1853, that John Ruskin (1819–1900) pointed out that architecture provides a just reflection of the moral life of a nation. Pawson's architecture reflects the luxurious simplicity of the vital thinking of the architect.

Ruskin distinguishes between architecture of structures and architecture of incrustations, two kinds of building and inhabiting that pervade European taste throughout its history. He distinguishes between architecture that emphasizes and considers as of primary importance the values of the articulation of spaces, tension and mass, and architecture that eulogizes the optical ensemble, the value of colour and of plastic effects, Rome versus Byzantium, simplicity of engineering, function and form versus cladding (mosaic, stained glass, etc.) In this tradition of Ruskin's criticism and thinking, Pawson sets out to combine both: the simplicity of the articulation of spaces, the engineering of proportion, with the touch of colour based on working with light. Light as energy and light as something fundamental, as in the simple linear work of Ben Nicholson recreating Italian architecture, or of Eduardo Chillida constructing reliefs.

This book is, I repeat, not a collection of plans or models or photographs taken with a wide-angle lens. Pawson has not used a chronological sequence in his architecture or the conventional media for representing architectural projects. The book marks out a survey of Pawson's work like Aby Warburg's visual atlas, a survey that juxtaposes general views and details of projects, underlining the simple ideas of constructing and inhabiting, where concepts such as scale, light or the significance of materials are the basis of his activity and his aesthetics.

This is a philosophical essay about building that lies between Zen and Minimalism. It is the voice of one of the great figures of modern architecture, represented as if in a series of *lieder*, a series of short songs. This book is an archaeology of knowledge or an iconographic memory that, for European architecture, revives ideas drawn from the Romanesque or from oriental cultures, a mixture that Warburg succeeded in discovering in the history of art in Renaissance Europe, in its iconography and in its vital significance.

Whether at the scale of a discrete architectural object such as a wash basin made from a single block of white Carrara marble, or of a complete building like the Calvin Klein store in Seoul, with its facade clad in the same stone used for the floor and entrance steps as well as the plinth on which it appears to sit, the idea of celebrating the qualities of mass is an essential part of John Pawson's approach to architecture.

The simplicity of the ideal geometric form of the basin – a perfect hemisphere – brings out the solidity and heft of its material, marble, in a way which acts as a foil to the fluidity of the water that it contains, running or still. Its mass gives it a powerful presence within any space, creating a dialogue with its architectural context that seems to create a sense of permanance, uniting contents with container.

The same celebration of mass as an architectural quality is something Pawson looks for on the larger scale as well. In the Cathay Pacific Lounges in Hong Kong's Chep Lap Kok airport, the massive dark granite entrance stairs that take passengers up through twin granite walls as massive as a cathedral provide a moment of transition away from the transience of the airport outside into the stillness of a sanctuary. The sense of compression that one experiences while rising up the stairs provides a powerful prelude to the open outlook of the lounge above under the undulating roof of Norman Foster's terminal building overhead. The solidity of the granite is emphasized by lighting at base level, heightening the texture of the stone and its materiality.

There is a similar effect with the Calvin Klein store in Seoul where the building rises seamlessly out of the ground almost as if it were a geological formation, side-stepping the impermanence that is the necessary accompaniment of fashion. It is a building that projects from the outside the sense of a perfect object, one that does not need to seduce passers by. It offers instead the refined attractions of its proportions, texture and sheer presence.

The Marketmuseum in Radcliffe in England also presents an inscrutable face, in this case as a unifying device that creates a cohesive setting for the diversity of the activities that take place within it: museum, galleries, market stalls and restaurants.

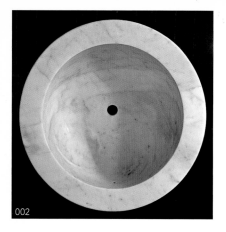

005

006

Who has not felt the seductive pull of a pool of sunshine on a floor in the near distance, beckoning with the promise of delicious heat? Light gives us not only the ability to distinguish one object from another, allowing us to make sense of the three-dimensional world, but often warmth as well. We associate it with well-being and prize it almost above all else in architecture. For the Incas, whose cosmology invested the natural world with religious signifigance, sunlight was the most powerful purifier. They believed it cleansed the soul and healed character defects that threatened the orderly working of their society.

The architect must use light with discrimination. Unshielded, its brightness floods our visual fields, destroying our ability to differentiate between elements in the physical realm, washing out all colour, causing pain to the optic nerve and eventual loss of function.

In John Pawson's hands, natural and artificial light are tools, part of his architectural arsenal, allowing him to focus attention and increase awareness. The light at the base of the wall in the lift core in the Cathay Pacific Lounges concentrates our attention on the act of joining a wall to a floor and the material used for each surface, stone.

The gentle skylighting in the Kerlin Gallery in Dublin provides even natural light for viewing art, while the combination of light from different directions in the living room of the Faggionato apartment emphasizes the proportions and volume of the space. The painterly play of sunlight on a window screen in the Miro house accentuates the border between inside and out, at once porous, protective and mysterious.

The skylight above the whole length of the stair in Pawson's own London house allows a shifting timeline along the walls, connecting a sense of the day's passage with the movement from floor to floor. The quiet white walls on one side of an otherwise unlit corridor in the Runkel Hue-Williams Gallery reflect spotlights mounted in the wood floor, providing a counterpoint to the even light of the gallery space ahead and giving the passageway a rhythm corresponding to the pace of the person walking through.

008

009

010

008
Lift core,
Cathay Pacific Lounges,
Chek Lap Kok Airport,
Hong Kong, 1998

009
Interior,
Runkel Hue-Williams Gallery,
London, 1988

010
Interior,
Miro House,
London, 1988

011
Living room,
Faggionato Apartment,
London, 1999

012
Remodelled interior,
Kerlin Gallery,
Dublin, 1994

011

012

013
Living room,
Tilty Barn,
Essex, 1995

John Pawson started designing in the early 1980s, a time when architectural discourse was dominated by brawny buildings that showed off their muscles, whether the mannered deconstructions of firms like Coop Himmelblau and Morphosis, or the articulated 'high-tech' buildings of Norman Foster and Richard Rogers. His architecture seemed to stand in cool contrast, as if arising from a different cultural context or set of assumptions. In Pawson's architecture structure is always a conscious element, revealed or hidden depending on an organic logic of hierarchy. We might look at the underside of a beautiful stone staircase and wonder how it can appear to float, unsupported. That question will not be answered in a way that we can trace physically, unless to do so will add something to our understanding of the space or to the pleasure we derive from being within it.

A round stone basin rests on a square pillar of the same material. The basin is off-centre, its underside curving out in implied response to the deflection of a body bent over it. Evidently the basin must have a considerable weight, yet it is easily cradled and supported by its column. The effort is revealed and rewarded: the two parts together create something that is both functional element and sculpture.

The doors in the Obumex kitchen swing open on stainless steel pivot hinges which are all but invisible when the doors are closed and unobtrusively hidden when they are open. They do not need to be noticeable in order to do their job effectively, so they are out of sight.

A column, its diameter equal to the width of the wall alongside it, anchors the open space of hall, kitchen and corridor in the van Royen apartment. The column is close enough to the wall beside it that the architect could have enclosed it, yet it stands on its own. Sometimes the best architectural response to structure must be to expose and work with what is already there. For the conversion of the eighteenth-century Tilty Barn into a modern habitation, Pawson chose to reveal the original wood frame structure for the walls and roof – a complex pattern of mostly hand-sawn and spaced timber. The effect is at once delicate and tough, the architectural equivalent of a dew-laden spider's web. In the Starkmann offices, Pawson inserted a series of white partitions which unify the space, giving what was once a chaotic jumble of rooms a sense of cohesion under one roof, each room flowing to the next.

The design for a watch factory for Vacheron Constantin reveals the structural bays that also organize the interior spaces on the exterior facade. It is a study in metronomic precision.

014

015

Structure

019
Garden,
Pawson House,
London, 1999

Rituals gain their power from the act of performance. Unlike the currency of ideas, they are not something that grows in value or importance by being taught, or read about, or discussed. It is the act of doing that we invest with significance. And it is through their repetition that they develop import – within the quiet opportunity to reflect on how iterations of a given ritual change from one to the next lies the potential for instruction.

Certain activities have an intrinsically ritualistic quality, such as the rites of religious practice. For others, the qualities associated with rituals are imbued by external factors. John Pawson presents us with a plinth for the display of items in the Calvin Klein store in Seoul. A witty altarpiece, it proffers items for our contemplation, selection and ultimate purchase, acknowledging the manner and rhythm of shopping. The dressing rooms in a store, such as the ones at Jigsaw on Bond Street in London, are our next stop in the performance of this particular ritual, the place where we change our garb and assume the personality implied by these garments.

Pawson judges every movement and activity for its fundamental components and potential for meaning. In one washroom that he designed, the long shallow sink, thin but very wide spout and contained water formally echo each other, working in concert. The bathroom in Tilty Barn has a freestanding bathtub in it and separates the acts of showering and bathing. Pawson's focus on designing space in a way that pays court to every action that will naturally occur in that space is in part the legacy of the time he spent living and working in Japan. His design for the kitchen in the Taira house is a meditation on how we nourish ourselves and how we connect to others. Even the way that a table is laid, like the outdoor one in the back garden of Pawson's London house, can be a conscious reflection on why and how we share our repasts. These activities are the rituals that give our lives shape. They are the considerations that Pawson brings together with outward ease to make spaces that seem perfectly suited to their functions.

020

021

022

020
Interior,
Calvin Klein Store,
Seoul, 1996

021
Washroom,
GAM Conference Suite,
London, 1995

022
Changing room,
Jigsaw Store,
London, 1996

023
Model,
Taira House,
Okinawa, (in progress)

024
Bathroom,
Tilty Barn,
Essex, 1995

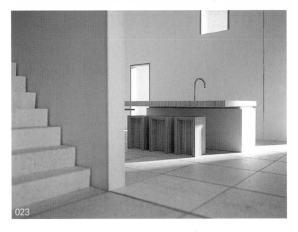

023

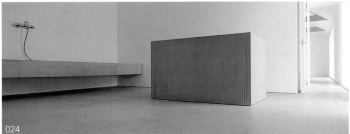

024

025
Rooftop,
Tunis House,
Tunis, 1995

Architecture can be an alchemical substance mediating the link between humanity and nature. The walls of the Neuendorf Villa, with their surface created in part from nearby soils, represent a version of the earth perfected and reflected back to its surroundings. The uneven ground underfoot has been made smooth and noble in these walls; the blue sky above claimed in the atrium as the rightful ceiling for this architecture of the land. The lap pool extends out from the building perpendicularly towards the horizon, a tongue of water mirroring the sky. Elements of nature are brought inside and ordered, so that they work harmoniously with the right angles and smooth planes of the building. Although they are tended, they are untamed, encouraged to retain their essential nature. In Pawson's architecture a channel of water might be used to create a boundary condition, one of sound as well as sight, as in the design for a private house in Germany.

Pawson captures the landscape in the distance and makes it part of the experience of his architecture, rising particularly to the challenge of how to bring a connection with the outdoors into an urban space. Steps lead down from a roof terrace in the Tunis house through a tall slot, framing a view of the cityscape beyond. A shower on the top storey of Pawson's own London house has a retractable roof, opening the room to the sky. The opening gives the room and the experience of showering there an intensely charged air. One feels like this is the centre of the universe, the ideal garden with indoor plumbing. In the front area of his house there is just enough room for a bench and an olive tree. The area has the tranquillity of a garden and the agreeable sense of enclosure of a room. It simultaneously offers the pleasures of being inside and out. A large piece of glass in a bedroom in Tilty Barn forms one of the walls. With no frame or edge detail, the window has the same architectural power and status as the three walls, working with them to provide shelter, although its role is to reveal as well.

026

027

028

029

030

031
Private working spaces,
Cathay Pacific Lounges,
Chek Lap Kok Airport,
Hong Kong, 1998

Everyone is an architecture critic. We grow up, work and live in buildings. We all have ample experience of architecture. But while the casual inhabitant can usually tell whether they like a space or not, they frequently have no idea why. In conversation we discuss architecture in terms of style, fashion, finish, period and provenance. But these are given deeper architectural meaning by an underlying and not always clearly expressed sense of order.

A circular white serving tray sits inside a square dark wooden one, its outer edge perfectly circumscribing the interior of its alter ego. Pawson's design for this element of the 'When Objects Work' collection derives its distinctive qualities from his complete understanding of what we want a tray, or two, to be. They are physical counterpoints that complement each other. They are each strong enough to be used alone, but light enough to be used in tandem.

Pawson brings an instinctive sense of order to all his projects, reconsidering received wisdom and searching for the essentials. In contemplating what a bedroom needed to be for the Abu Saad apartment, he decided that a private space with natural light and enough room for a futon, rolled up and stored during the day when not required, was not just enough, but exactly right. It is a response that may seem austere, but is reasoned and measured. The same reductive process is evident in the chapter house of Novy Dvur. There the monks will meet to discuss and conduct monastery business. The single volume is all it needs to be. No architectural gestures are wasted and no energy squandered.

Translucent screens at Jigsaw divide the season's collection into manageable groups. Long display racks hold garments organized by type in short perpendicular rows for simpler selection. Order may come through modulation. The Cathay Pacific Lounges overlook the busy airport interior and runways, providing a sense of calm in the middle of the bustle of Chep Lap Kok, itself a veritable twenty-four hour city. In the van Royen apartment, a 100 foot long wall connects the gallery, library and sitting areas at the front with the dining room and kitchen at the back. Monolithic freestanding walls subdivide the apartment and create smaller private rooms.

032

033

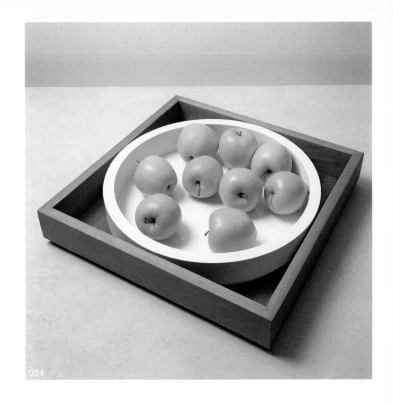

037
Interior,
Calvin Klein Store,
New York, 1995

A building's first role is to shelter us from the elements. Defence from the hardships of weather alone however constitutes neither architecture nor the fulfilment of our need for refuge. While the desire for simple containment is instinctive in some creatures (many animals will burrow in the wild for shelter) human yearnings are much more complex.

The mezzanine in the Faggionato apartment has children's bedrooms above and shelters the dining room set behind a dark glass wall. Containment and openness reinforce each other through the consideration of what is done best where. The ramped vitrines of the Boilerhouse exhibition at the Victoria and Albert Museum of 1984 were wedges that held objects. Through their shape and placement, these vitrines forced visitors to move their bodies into crouched positions at times so that the full array of items on display could be seen. Through their form they provoked a necessary physical response from the visitor. A curved glass wall fronts on to a busy road in the Wakaba restaurant in London. The opaque coloured wall shifts the point of entry from the standard front door onto the street to a side door just perpendicular to it. Inside, the glass wall glows while shielding diners from the noise and bustle of the busy roadway.

Other pleasures are improved by a sense of enclosure as well. In the Calvin Klein store in New York the tall walls have niches carved out at ground level for the display of clothing. The entrance to the Calvin Klein store in Tokyo is like a decompression chamber, allowing the shopper to walk in off the busy street and concentrate on the quiet and luxurious clothing and surroundings. The kitchen sink in Pawson's own London house is designed as an extension of the countertop worksurface, one that can usefully contain water.

038

039

040

041

042

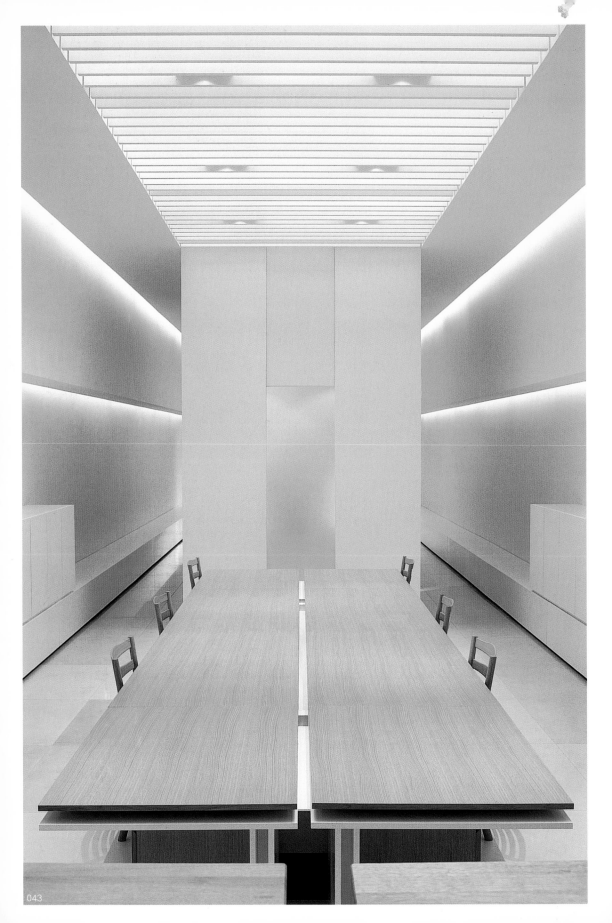

043
Bulthaup showroom,
London, 2001

Science-fiction writers dream up worlds in which objects, houses, cities, people, are cloned, with endlessly repeated versions of the same thing. The effect is often calculated to frighten, as if the loss of (heroic) individuality were at stake. Yet without similarity we cannot know difference. And repetition is simply comforting. Who does not have a favourite food, or view, or piece of music, something sought out or returned to again and again for its ability to soothe and thereby delight? The richness and texture of our lives increases dramatically from these successive forays, a kind of repetition over both time and space.

In the Cathay Pacific Lounges in Hong Kong, John Pawson created both the Long Bar overlooking the runways and generous individual spaces, each with a comfortable armchair, table and phone. They are small-scale refuges, providing a temporary place of rest for the individual traveller. Pawson's design for Jigsaw on Bond Street in London includes a series of etched acrylic screens on both floors, used to divide the store into discrete spaces where shelves and rails display groups of clothing.

The Bulthaup showroom in London has an intentionally mute facade, revealing nothing about what is inside. The interior is the realm of theatre and imagination, with products displayed in distinct symmetrical groups that allow one to contemplate how they might look and function in one's own home. In the Faggionato apartment the children's bedrooms are identical cells successively arranged down the length of the mezzanine, with a long desk outside that unifies the space and gives the children room to work.

Sometimes it is the function that is repeated in the spatial elements, as in the ground floor and courtyard in the house on Rosmead Road. A table sits in the centre of the courtyard, the same scale as the one in the house just the other side of the glass wall. Weather permitting, the Pawson family can enjoy the same activities out of doors as in. In the nineteenth-century Dean Clough complex in Halifax, Pawson's renovation of the space included the stripping out of twentieth-century additions which obscured the original beauty and order. Each column is a delight of Victorian engineering and building. To see them in their repeated glory now is to be able to appreciate their enduring aesthetic value.

Repetition

049
Interior,
250 Brompton Road,
London, 2001

Without careful consideration of programme and usage, sheer volume means little. The Calvin Klein store in New York is in a space that formerly housed a bank, complete with vault. John Pawson opened the streetscape with the largest pieces of glass commercially available in the United States, then inserted a mezzanine floor that steps back from the facade. The effect is a light-filled space whose soaring grandeur comes from the careful interplay of levels and volumes. At 250 Brompton Road, Pawson took a long and narrow site and gave it a low curved roof with a skylight that emphasizes the length, selectively opening the interior to the sky. The space has the kind of quality of strength and stillness that comes from the control of motion. The volumetric swell is horizontal rather than vertical, but relies on proportion just the same.

The bowl from the 'When Objects Work' collection is a perfect hemisphere both inside and out, that can rest in any position along its continuously curved surface. Tactile and ingenious, it is at once a volume in space and a vessel that can contain. Each new angle of footing is a unique event. John Pawson's architecture office in London ranges over two levels. While the entrance is at street level, the main floor is in the basement of an industrial building now converted to mixed usage. Pawson opened the space by removing part of the ground floor, thus creating a mezzanine level and a generous volume for the main area. Even in the basement, the Pawson office is light-filled and airy. It is an exercise in the careful modulation of compression and volumetric expansion, particularly apt in an architect's office.

The double-height volume of the entrance to the Jigsaw store on Bond Street and the width of the display area allows the mannequins to show off their wares at a pace transformed by the quality of the space. In the Tunis house, an outdoor stairwell leads to the roof terraces. The tall narrow space is the height of the house, unrelieved by openings except to the sky above.

050

051

052

43

Volume

053

054

055
Vase,
John Pawson for
When Objects Work,
Belgium, 2001

There is a point with every experience, object and idea, where nothing more can be added or taken away without lessening its intensity. Finding that point is not simply a matter of applying Ockham's razor. One might work accretionally in order to create that point of natural harmony where the sum is greater than the parts and the elements fuse, losing their own identity.

Spaces for art must necessarily defer to what they show, yet architecture is not a blank canvas. No space is merely neutral. The spatial grace of the Michael Hue-Williams Gallery is evident in the way the architecture seems absent. Like the perfect servant, it exists only to serve its master's wants and needs.

The designs of the waterspout and handles of the Obumex kitchen are a fusion of form and function. The waterspout, with its graceful arc, precisely describes the shape of water moving through space, but made real and fixed in metal. It seems so appropriate and natural as to be inevitable. Pawson's bathtubs, whether made from wood or stone, are often freestanding and always single-purpose. They are an invitation to immerse one's body in water. Luscious and full, the experience of bathing oneself in such a tub might have the power to cleanse the psyche as well as the body.

The Cathay Pacific Lounges have a water channel that runs through them, bounded by a translucent glass wall separating public areas from personal ones. The water channel creates a gentle and soothing boundary of sound. In combination with the glass wall it creates rippling reflections and shadows, visible from spaces that range in level of privacy from the Long Bar that overlooks the runways to individual bathrooms and lounging areas for first class customers. It integrates spaces with diverse functions.

The vase for the 'When Objects Work' collection is a clear acrylic volume that houses a metal sheath within its core. The prominence of the inner container depends on the angle of viewing. The design of the vase exemplifies the exact point of ideal restraint for a vessel for flowers, themselves the essence of natural beauty.

056

057

Essence

056
Water channel,
Cathay Pacific Lounges,
Chek Lap Kok Airport,
Hong Kong, 1998

057
Bath,
Pawson House,
London, 1994

058
Handles,
John Pawson for Obumex,
Belgium, 1996

059
Spout,
John Pawson for Obumex,
Belgium, 1996

060
Front window,
Michael Hue-Williams Gallery,
London, 1996

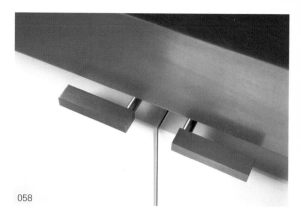

058

059

060

061
Window,
Cannelle Cake Shop,
London, 1988

Architecture and design speak without words. As social artefacts, they tell us something about history and economics. Architecture can have great clarity and eloquence of expression about how our lives are and how we wish they were.

The stepped threshold and square cut-out through a thick wall in the van Royen apartment create a transition that is simultaneously horizontal and vertical, physically articulating the division between the two main rooms. The floor appears seamless through them, a polished ebony surface. The architecture communicates something to us in the passage from one room to another about their symbiotic relationship. The sky shower created by the retractable roof in Pawson's London house reminds us that modern indoor plumbing is after all an attempt to control and refine nature, for what is a shower if not the simulacrum of rain? The rich and unusual combination of glass, stone, and wood in the Rothman apartment, all highly tactile but individual, materially mark the changing function from sleep and repose to cleansing and grooming.

The storefront of the Cannelle Cake Shop is opaque, with just enough room to display a single cake, made all the more alluring for being by itself. A gorgeous confection, self-consciously proud that it is not essential nourishment, is displayed without reference to any of the other wares within. We know this cake, revelling in its frivolity, was made to satisfy desire, not hunger.

The bathroom in Pawson's first London house is all stone except for the fixtures. It is a room completely free of visual distraction. Water drains through the floor. With a bench for lying down or sitting in the shower, it is the architectural idealization of each experience one might have in such a room. The stairs, with treads and risers of Douglas Fir without a visible joint or lip, rise with perfect geometry to a light-filled landing. Each journey up such a staircase must feel like a metaphysical act, a consideration of the relationship between the journey and the end.

064

062

065

063

062
Stairs,
Pawson House,
London, 1994

063
Glass screens,
Rothman Apartment,
London, 1990

064
Interior,
van Royen Apartment,
London, 1986

065
Bathroom,
Pawson House,
London, 1994

066
Sky shower,
Pawson House,
London, 1999

066

Respect for the inherent qualities of materials is one of the most decisive elements in the creation of powerful architecture.

Pawson prefers to use the same materials inside and out where possible. To do so is to avoid the junctions between one material and another that stop the eye. For the floor of his first London house Pawson used Douglas Fir from Denmark long enough to run the entire length of the house without the need for any distracting end-to-end joints between pieces. The effect is of a poured surface, yet made of wood. The table and benches are also made of Douglas Fir.

Metal can be made into a plane of almost any shape and dimension. One of the options Pawson designed for the countertop and sink of the Obumex kitchen is a continuous steel surface. The metal flows seamlessly from the worktop into the sink. The steel surface is patternless and non-reactive, making it ideal for a kitchen.

The glass wall at Wakaba, enigmatic and glowing, provides an ambiguous kind of shelter. It is not a barrier but a filter whose character depends upon the degree of transparency. Curved panels of translucent acid-etched glass preserve the privacy of the interior and yet offer a sense of the animate nightlife of the city outside.

In the Calvin Klein store in New York Pawson uses stone as a seamless surface. Durable and enduring, the choice of York stone reduces the need for different materials and awkward junctions between them, as the stone can be used for fittings as well. The long stone plinths rise up, monolithic, like extrusions of the floor.

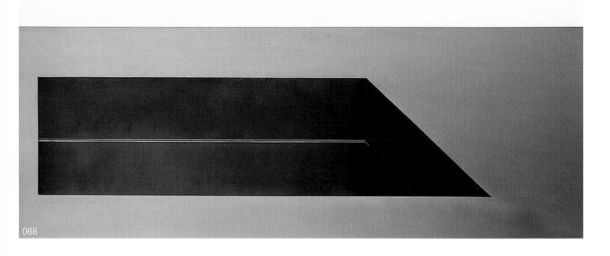

068

069

068
Sink,
John Pawson for Obumex,
Belgium, 1996

069
Calvin Klein Store,
New York, 1995

070
Wakaba Restaurant,
London, 1987

070

Self-taught architecture by definition can hardly be a tradition. By its nature it is a category of practice that implies a fresh invention of the subject through personal discovery that is different for each individual. But there are a number of architects who are perhaps not quite entirely self-taught and who, despite their impact on the conventional architectural profession, have never been part of it. Conventional practice is not simply a matter of possessing a professional diploma. It involves a mind-set, in which the exigencies of maintaining a professional office become an end in itself, rather than a means to an end. And that involves jostling for intellectual position as well as for work, two sides of the same thing in fact. Architecture in this sense is both defined and circumscribed by a shared language, developed to protect turf and exclude interlopers. Avoiding a conventional training and membership of professional institutes does not constitute a school or a movement, but it does seem to give those who continue to build without them a certain amount in common. It's not a question of skills, but of shared assumptions that mark them out from the mainstream. Carlo Scarpa and Jean Prouvé, Pierre Chareau and Tadao Ando, Eileen Gray and Luis Barrágan and Craig Ellwood share a certain emotional intensity. Much of their work has been on a relatively small scale. It may have had its roots in domestic projects. But in the hands of such architects, the individual house can be seen more as a vision for a way of life than simply as an issue of form-making or pragmatism. While most of them moved on to larger projects, the transition has in some cases been a testing process. Coming closer to the mainstream while retaining a distinctive voice is not always easy. The self-taught learn by doing, but they do not necessarily limit their ambitions to the quality and craft of making. They have the chance to make discoveries and connections from more unexpected sources, and to transgress conventional boundaries between disciplines.

John Pawson, while he did study briefly at the Architectural Association when he was in his thirties, has the sense of freshness in his work that comes from thinking every move in every piece of architecture he makes as if he were doing it all for the first time. He began to practise in a way that was clearly somewhat outside the architectural mainstream. His decisions about architectural design are made not on the basis of precedent or ideology, but rather are based on a more personal vision. Materials, space and movement are considered without professional or historical baggage. That is what gave his first projects the shocking quality of a cold-water drenching. He was offering not the conventional simplicity of modernism, but a distillation of a series of ideas about space, about possessions and about a way of life. Ludwig Wittgenstein with his single house in Vienna seems to have been more of a model than was a conventional professional career. To make architecture himself was initially the accidental outcome of a line of intellectual inquiry. Pawson only began to consider the possibilities of taking on the role of an architect after a series of commissions with Shiro Kuramata came to nothing. Rather than watching others, why not design for himself, Kuramata suggested. The first few projects established a territory for Pawson which ushered him into the arena of architecture on his own account. He established an office that operated more like the network of assistants that an artist might maintain to realize his work than a traditionally organized design studio. Despite that, Pawson managed to bring about a shift in the architectural landscape with work that had the ability to propel those who experienced it into a different world-view. The images of restraint and sensuous austerity of the constantly photographed early galleries and apartments burned their way into the global image bank, appealing directly over the head of the architectural world to a wider popular consciousness. It's not that Pawson was making architecture that was attempting to be art. But his was architecture that had the potential to move people at both a physical and intellectual level, to consider aspects of space and materials from a different perspective. Pawson was not so much inventing an architectural language as rediscovering and reassembling a series of fragments from disparate sources that taken together suddenly put into sharp focus a view of the world. He made visible what had been previously hidden in plain sight. He was pointing out, let's say, the parallels between Cistercian monasteries, Shaker furniture and Mies van der Rohe. Even in the smallest of his spaces, Pawson seemed to be offering a complete conceptual blueprint for an architectural language. This was not a formula, but an attitude, one which Pawson went on to develop on public commissions that transcended the dimensions of the early work.

Of course nothing happens in isolation. In retrospect what Pawson was doing could be seen as part of a wider shift in sensibility that looked for alternatives to the decorative distractions of architecture as it was practiced in the postmodern years. In several parts of the world, architects independently began an exploration of ordinariness and the everyday in a search for an architecture of profundity undistracted by formal gymnastics, technological alibis or decorative excess. Like Pawson, they were trying to turn down the noise level, and let thickness and volume, clarity and restraint be heard for what they are. Others were self-consciously attempting to revive the vocabulary of the early modernists, a *rappel à l'ordre* in the language of Mies van der Rohe. Pawson's references did not come from the strand of fourth-hand Bauhaus ideology that continued to shape most architectural education into the 1980s, or an innocent belief in the redemptive possibilities of functionalism, or architecture as problem-solving.

Pawson was certainly not proposing the social programme of modernity. His view of architecture is not proselytizing, or offering a social utopia. He is much too polite, much too English to look for converts. His work is essentially a personal project which he is ready to share but not to palm off on the uninitiated or the reluctant. The unexpected thing about Pawson's work is just how much impact it has had despite its restricted quantity and the essentially private nature of its domestic components. Its power is in its startling beauty and its ability to communicate. That it is based on a sense of direction has a powerful attraction at a moment in which architecture seems to lack a roadmap.

Architecture is inevitably part of a wider system of fluctuations in perception and fashion. Pawson's example has been followed by designers around the world. More or less successfully, Minimalism became a fleetingly fashionable idea. Once the word was coined it became possible to lump together architects with not very much in common, simply on the basis of their interest in concrete – not in fact a material that Pawson has made much use of – or their adoption, mannerist-style, of certain fetishistic details: the apotheosis of the shadow gap, the floating bench, the stone bath. But Pawson's work has a robustness that allows it to transcend the trivialization of the label. Crucially, he has demonstrated the ability to move on in his work, to make scale shifts, from individual apartments, gallery spaces and remodelling to individual houses, then to more public commissions, a theatre, a factory, offices, that begin to take on directly urban issues as well as spatial and emotional ones.

It's hard to imagine a more angelic designer than John Pawson. I mean this not in the sense of him being a heavenly figure, but because his work seems more part of the sky than the ground. Even when he re-examines the kitchen and its complex functions, or re-evaluates the essence of a Victorian house, he seems not to concern himself with material as presence, but material as ideas. Floating ideas.

Like Pawson, I spent many years living in Japan – not the uniform skyscrapers and coloured neon lights Japan, but a small house, a very small house. It was in a narrow street where all the doors are small and with no locks, old people living side by side with youngsters, each house connected by telephone wires. The house was made of simple materials – wood, glass and paper – and it allowed the seasons to enter it rather than insulating from them. The entrance was small, with a place to change into sandals, leading to the main room consisting of Tatami – used for sleeping, dining and entertaining. Storage was kept out of sight, concealed by light sliding doors. The bath was a square container set on bricks, so that water could overflow naturally. Its simplicity became therapeutic, an antidote to the electronic landscape just a few hundred yards away. If this sounds like a *gaijin* (foreigner) attempting to live the life of old Japan, then you are mistaken. I was not so interested in living the life of a Japanese person (most of my friends' homes were exercises in extreme packing, which typifies contemporary Tokyo) but it felt right that the necessities of life were not in the objects that might populate our rooms, but in the surfaces that my body was to touch or to lean against. I had become a minimalist not out of choice, or trend, but in the belief that what was required was in fact very little. And so here is the conundrum. If little is required, what role does a designer or architect then have? For Pawson I believe that it is to make the purpose of the seemingly 'little' the most great. When it comes to objects or the things we touch, it is their reason for existence that is the joy itself. Pawson exercises this thinking by making the essence of the work shine through, with a subtlety that invites discovery rather than intrusion.

There is another designer who once shared this ability to understand the things in life that words cannot describe. It was Shiro Kuramata, and it is no coincidence that Pawson spent time with him. Kuramata believed that design was not about what material we might see or touch, but what ideas or feelings transcend to our hearts and mind. To this end, Kuramata's palette moved from what we see, to what we touch, to what we think – constantly at play with each other. He lived not in a black and white world, but a grey world, a world where there was no clear right or wrong. His work always relied upon the human being to complete the picture, to form the essential 'ah' notion. It was when one of his objects was used intuitively that it became so understandable as to feel ghostly and awesome. Always floating and never grounded. The tension between experimentation with materiality and the effect that it has with our mind is a quality that differentiates simplicity as an execution of simple reduction from simplicity that shows ideas beyond the material. This poetry of thinking and aptitude is not something that can necessarily be studied. I have always felt that Kuramata's influence lives in John Pawson's work, and it was reaffirmed to me in his latest collection 'When Objects Work'. But I shall come to these in a moment.

The Obumex Kitchen, designed in 1999, is an example of how what we see is not what we should feel. It is where this tension between materiality and feeling is played out. To look at the kitchen, we might find it sharp, cold and heavy, the same that can be seen in a typical Japanese kitchen in a factory building on the outskirts of Osaka. But what we feel is liberating, clear and inquisitive. This oddity of contrast between what we see and feel is central to much of Pawson's work. The Obumex spout is nothing more than a stainless steel pipe, bent towards the sink. This might be what we see, but we feel pleased that this pipe fits our dreams of what a spout should look like. Even when it is turned off, we imagine the water travelling along its length. Even though we have not seen a spout like it, this is what a spout must really look like. Whether a peasant or a wealthy merchant, this spout is of the same dream. And it results from the skill and determination of someone like Pawson, who is able not only to see the essential, but also to remove all compromise in its execution.

For his recent collection 'When Objects Work', Pawson turned to the notion of before and after. One such item is the Bowl, which has a clear gestural elegance of being in use and a floating quality when empty. The thick profile appears at first heavy and solid, but its thickness has reasoning far beyond the aesthetic. It allows a cavity in its wall thickness to contain sand, and it is this material that, although unseen, turns the bowl into an animated object.
As you tilt it, the sand maintains its position, allowing the bowl to stay tilted. Most bowls that we see, whether European or Chinese, have a base that allows them to stand on a table surface. From the side profile, the base can change the purity of the containing form into something else. The designer is aware that a bowl is seen from all directions, yet few are designed to be seen this way. If there is one exquisite idea in Pawson's Bowl, it is that he has managed to maintain the simplicity of the bowl's profile whilst not removing any of the aesthetic functional requirements that another bowl might have. The base is now internal, via the sand. The base becomes invisible.
The result – a floating container, with a reassessment of the tension between object and table surface.

For Pawson, material is as much about the intangible as the tangible – the tension between the expectation of the mind and the discovery of the real.

The artist Michael Craig-Martin has long been intimately familiar with John Pawson's work and ideas. Their fruitful and on-going dialogue included the design by Pawson of Craig-Martin's studio in 1988. The following is an excerpt from a conversation about the interrelationship between art and architecture ten years later.

John Pawson: So much is made these days of minimalism across different disciplines. I want to talk about what influences the impact of a piece of art in a domestic space.

Michael Craig-Martin: A lot of people make different kinds of attempts at minimalist ideas about architecture but people seem to think it has to do simply with not having many things. It seems to me it has more to do with whether a design concept actually deals with defining the space or not. If you've got a room with not very much in it, it can be just boring. If, on the other hand, the creation of space has been made visible, that can be very interesting. Art responds better when it is in the context of a space that has genuine character. And I think you can have real character in a space that is very simple or in a space that is very complex.

JP: Do you think the scale of the work of art matters in that context? I'm thinking of when I went to see what Donald Judd had created in Marfa. I was just wandering around and noticed that Judd had a small Rembrandt, a quite small, very dark etching of a head, about a foot square. He had it in one of the studios in town where there was a rural mural; essentially, it was just in a room somewhere. It was obviously hung carefully. The etching affected me powerfully when I came on it because it was so unexpected, in a sense. So it was a very potent experience, even before I realised that it was a Rembrandt.

MC-M: Rembrandts are amazing little objects, small yet with immense intensity. When you talk about space in architecture you are talking about the phenomenological experience of the space. When I wake up in the morning I'm immediately struck by how beautiful this space is. I can see this space, it isn't an invisible backdrop. And my sense of my own physicality in the world is reinforced by recognizing that I'm in a space that is defined in a special

way. Works of art can have so much physical presence, the tiny Rembrandt etching can have the same impact without being three-dimensional, or big, or brightly coloured. If you have great intensity in a small object it radiates its own energy. There's a certain way in which really good works of art, even when they are tiny like the Rembrandt, are assertive. I'm always very struck by that, for example if you talk about an Agnes Martin drawing, something incredibly refined, very slight – it's precisely because its modest physicality is so heightened that I think it's very successful. There is also an issue about how art works in a domestic scale. The National Gallery is wonderful, and there are hundreds of marvellous pieces of art, but if you go to somebody's house with just a couple of fabulous things it's almost more incredible. One can see how truly strong something is when it works in those circumstances.

JP: For me, anything that you hang on the wall affects the space. Unfortunately, so often in a negative way.

MC-M: Yes, I think that's true. But it's important to realise that architectural space is a product of its era. If you have a space of the kind that you design in which there was only one work, and that one work was a Rembrandt, it would affect the space in a way that was essentially contemporary – it would act like a contemporary artwork because your concept of space is not a seventeenth or eighteenth-century concept of space. How we think about space and how space is used has changed. That is as true of architecture as it is of art. If you put a work of art from that period into a contemporary space that artwork is naturally made more contemporary. And how art is hung in a room has changed as well. If you have a room with a single object obviously that focuses tremendous attention on it. It can be a very rewarding experience as an inhabitant of that room, because you really do learn about something by being asked to look at it. That's a very modern idea. One of the things that came up in the discussions with Herzog and de Meuron about the Tate was the question of how to make spaces that accept a lot of different things yet aren't neutral. Sometimes minimal is taken as a kind of neutral. I go to a lot of spaces these days that are very plain without many things in them. They are very simple, and in that sense they are minimal, but in fact the space is completely dead. It's not made alive by this simplification. And many museums are boring architecturally within the galleries. Very often the public spaces, the staircases, the restaurants, the bookshops may be quite interesting while the galleries are strangely bland. If you go into a great building, and most people never have the experience of going into a really great piece of architecture, certainly not a really great twentieth-century piece of architecture, there is something about the way that experience captivates people, they are slightly overwhelmed by it. It's about the experience of being alive. And it's not just that it's modern. I always think it's incredibly exciting when people see things for the first time. I think that's one of the reasons there is a great deal of contemporary interest in the Tate and in the most recent art. That's why people go and see the Turner Prize: even when people are critical or are aware that the work is very current, people want that experience because it gives them an intense sense of contemporaneity which very few things give you.

JP: Art has a tremendous power to charge architecture and change our understanding of space, but that is usually limited in the way that people relate to art in their own homes. In a gallery context shows open and close and the art changes, and our understanding of the space transforms along with it. At home, on the other hand, most people don't change their art.

MC-M: Yes, I think most people hang a picture over the mantelpiece and think 'Well that's done, I don't have to worry about that again'. They want a sense of continuity, but in effect the picture disappears. It becomes bland and a part of the total ambience of the room. Whereas if you have a room in which you have very powerful works of art and it's there for a month, six months, a year, it gives you a very intense experience. Removing it and replacing it with something else changes the whole nature of that experience and place. Ideally that's what I hope to be able to do here in my own studio. I'd like to have a sense of impermanence with great depth, in that one looks at

something intensely, but only for a period of time. I come to this question from the point of view of an artist, and to me that is the contemporary equivalent to the way in which the spaces that you design would have their ideal relation to art.

'So when's the furniture arriving?'
A question I have heard many times, having lived in four Pawson homes over twenty-three years. Met often with a sense of pride in knowing that the flat could still pull off the old tricks. That it was still different, unusual. That, I too, as child of this house was also, somehow, a little different. Not that, until much more recently, I was ever really conscious of inhabiting a space that some people might classify as odd, unnatural or, as Janet Street Porter described it, 'smooth, vacant, vacuous, unreal'. 'Smooth', yes it was and that was always a good thing – no other house anywhere had 100 ft of pure sock-sliding potential. 'Vacant', well there weren't many objects around – lucky really, considering I was queen cartwheeler of the world and my brother was the next Maradona. 'Vacuous', never. 'Unreal', right, so it was all a fiction. No, above all else, it always just felt like home.

I suppose I should explain that John was not just the architect of my various childhood homes, but also my mother's partner for ten years. I was a child of a Pawson home in more than one sense. Our first home together was a small flat in Elvaston Place that my mother was renting. Even before John's arrival, it was what one would call minimal – white walls, rush matting on the floor, the only furniture a glass table with OMK plastic furniture that my mother thought was the height of sophistication. What John's arrival did was, as my mother describes it in retrospect, to articulate her taste, to fine-tune it through the details. What actually happened was that she came home one day to find the flat completely gutted – the old interior a mass of rubble in the middle of the front room and floating about as dust in the air. Creating design history in reality meant having to live amongst debris and midnight escapades to dispose of the evidence, lugging it out in plastic bags and carting it off in her new car. The final result, though, must have been worth it, as my mother can't remember being too angry after her initial, 'oh my God, what have you done?' Instead, what she remembers is loving the four years that were spent there and managing to pacify the landlord with each new piece that came out in a magazine, as another nought was added to the value of the property.

My childhood homes are recorded in various powerful photographs. There is the famous shot of a huge, bloody T-bone steak, (or was it a white rabbit?) stretched out over the kitchen counter. In another in the same sequence, my mother, John and I stand behind the counter, unsmiling, dressed in black and white. Do these rather severe images capture the reality of life in a Pawson flat? Not quite. Actually not at all. We lived in colour, with laughter, and all meat was cooked. And not one of us, ever, killed a rabbit and laid it trophy-like across the kitchen table.

My first room was a small platform suspended a few feet above the ground, that could only be reached by a stepladder. I remember thinking this was very cool – as a pirate I was fiercely proud of my riggings. Some, though, like my aunt, seemed to find it a very odd existence. As far as she was concerned, I was secreted away in a sepulchre of tidiness and gloom. The seeming lack of mess, to her, meant that I wasn't being able to develop properly. There was, of course, mess; it was just contained mess. The one rule of all our flats was that you could do what you like in your room, but everything outside must be cleared up straight away.

The next house is a succession of pictures in my head – bar stools and poached eggs, endless roller-skating in the alley outside my room; the running-away bag hidden at the top of my cupboard – not so hidden it couldn't be found and asked about; cartwheeling everywhere; neon Nauman signs splashing green and pink all over the walls; the arrival of my brother; and the departure of John.

Certain memories are common to all of the Pawson houses in which I have lived – staring at the incredible sunsets, loving my friends' reactions when they saw the floor-to-ceiling doors for the first time, hating the silence then growing to love it, observing how perfectly a door becomes part of an abstract geometric composition when swung open and parallel to the wall, how light and shadows congregate endlessly on every surface, how everything goes blue and shapes seem diffuse as dusk descends, how all thoughts seem absolutely lucid when you are in one of those spaces and the longer you stare at the white walls the more worlds and ideas are revealed.

It is a truism that we make the places and then the places make us, but like most truisms, there is truth in it. I do know that I won't be living in a space quite like those I grew up in for some time – at least until I can afford high ceilings and a cleaner.

Even from the road the house looks unusual. It forms one half of a quaint two-door terrace which seems to have slipped its mooring and come to rest halfway down one of the northern slopes of Notting Hill. In an area of smart terraced crescents, all trim stucco and period cornices, the two houses seem a touch forlorn and erratic – like stray boulders dropped by some glacial commotion in the Victorian property market. Their curious position gives them handsome and enviable views along the two tongues of communal garden on either side, but they feel temporary: their exposed flanks, unmarked by so much as a window, suggest that they are lost, that they expect one day to rediscover their rightful place in the confusing local jigsaw of terraces from which they have somehow strayed.

Nevertheless, the house presents an urbane formal front to the world, modestly donning standard Victorian-terrace uniform – the architectural equivalent of black tie – for its dealings with the outside world. John Pawson has illuminated this by internalizing his drainage pipes and polishing his exterior walls. From the outside the house looks smooth: nothing spills out. But walk behind – not easy, since the garden is private – and everything changes. The rear has been cut away and replaced by glass. Light gushes into a soft courtyard where it creates a golden cube of wood and stone wrapped, like a gift, with wisteria, clematis and honeysuckle. As with all house plots that back on to a communal garden, the sober front is a folly, a *trompe l'œil*, a mere brass plate. If it were a toy, you would think that someone had prised the back off: you can see rooms and stairs, floors and walls. The house stands on the road, but does not look that way. Its focus is fixed on the green acres behind, where frost falls in winter and where, in summer, willows, cherries and ash trees cast cool shadows over the bright lawn, where foxes cry at night and where bikes litter the gravel footpath.

Rus in urbe, as they say: the country within the town. This has been and remains a classic residential ideal: the best of both worlds – the excitement and pressure of a city, plus trees and grass, daffodils and roses. By a small freak of social history (the crescents in these parts echo the curves of a Victorian racecourse: the Ladbroke Hippodrome) a rare and expensive few furlongs of green have survived the decades of blitz, demolition and zoning. For the houses that surround it the communal back garden is literally the focus – the point where their gazes meet. Residents lock their front doors and throw open the back, arranging their chairs to address the trees.

Everyone knows that an Englishman's house is his castle: the fantasy of private property is one of our most entrenched national reflexes. But in these placid squares the time-honoured quest for privacy, for Virginia Woolf's famous 'room of one's own', has been summarily abandoned. The formal frontage still functions as a fortress, a wall to keep the street and the vibrant clamour of city life at bay. But what looks from the road like a stiff, buttoned-up terrace becomes, seen from the garden, a relaxed and varied open gallery of domestic scenes. Here, contradicting almost every sacred principle of housing, the outside spills in.

The backs of these homes are glassy – some visitors react in horror, imagining this to be life in a goldfish bowl – which means that the boundaries between the interior life and the outer world are blurred. And by clearing the way for the houses to gaze onto the garden, the houses themselves are opened up to the gaze from the garden. Occasionally a bird or a cat will hop indoors; a squirrel might tap at a window. On summer nights it is like a camping site. Candles glimmer through barbecue smoke, glass clinks on glass, and there are sudden bursts of music and chatter in the gloom. But the gardens also have a monastic quality: to stroll the perimeter path at dusk beneath the tall trees, rising to the sky like spires, is rather like taking a turn around a cloister.

And this cheerful schizophrenia neatly inverts the historic priorities of private life. In the past, the smart rooms used to be at the front: this was where visitors were received and formal occasions celebrated. Life's messier business was conducted out back, out of sight. The houses on communal gardens reverse this formula: the functional stuff – washing machines, cupboards for coats and boots, kitchens and bathrooms – tends to be tucked at the front, and the living space gathers around the view. The garden hosts two social events each year: a fireworks party on bonfire night, and a summer party with races for the children and a marquee for their dancing parents. At these times the houses become pavilions, a ring of balconies overlooking the fun on the grass forum outside.

The desire to acquire the landscape and its horizon, the urge to do away with neighbours altogether, is another pressing British fantasy, as old as the hills. Mature gardens, rolling lawns, vistas of lordly oaks, ha-has and ornamental lakes – how grand it would be to dwell in such style. But the communal garden behind the house fractures this greedy aristocratic ideal by flinging open each house to its neighbours'. Indeed, though the residents are not even remotely communists, the arrangement of their houses represents an élite form of communal living. This remains an exclusive, private space: the houses are wagons drawn into a circle to form a privileged haven for those who can afford them. In earlier times this is where they might have kept sheep or goats, or grown turnips. Now they stroll around with dogs, or, if they are young, spray each other with water pistols and kick footballs into the trees to bring the conkers down. Either way, neighbourliness is a fact, not a quality of life. And it cuts both ways. It is easy enough to borrow a bottle of milk or a cup of sugar. But give them your rising damp and they may sue you. The delicious golden courtyard, which in repose gives off whiffs of Mediterranean verandas (you half expect to glimpse blue sea through the surrounding latticework) is popular among the garden's under-tens as a basketball court. John himself was woken once at dawn to find a young child (mine) by his bed, demanding to see his puppy.

A sense of community – what a political cliché! Yet this is precisely the quality that modern cities find hardest to cultivate. Bohemian rebels, poets and runaways all cluster in the city to escape the glare of publicity in the suburbs. Each, passing unnoticed through the terrific swarm of other people, sees not other individuals but only a vague crowd. The result of this, in cities, is that we tend to express our individuality

most vividly when we are in. When we are out and about we simply join the tidal motion of masses drifting to and fro; only in the so-called privacy of our own homes do we give in to display – to decor and design and the symbolic statements we wish to make about ourselves. Our shelves reveal our selves.

This is especially true of a communal garden. We are never more exposed than when we are at home. Neighbours might drop in: their children certainly will. Step outside and we might find ourselves helping someone lug a table upstairs, or we could be handed a cup of coffee or a glass of wine. The interior of John Pawson's house recognizes this in a profound and wholehearted way. By stashing the details of private life – books, videos, plates and glasses, clothes and toys – behind cupboard doors, the whole house becomes a display case. But a display case for people, not for things: there are no trophies on the shelves, no pictures on the walls. Sit in the kitchen or in the levantine reception room upstairs, and you are flanked by two huge organic landscapes: the views on either side. Tiptoe down the path out back and, looking in, you see a still-life – a domestic scene in perfect perspective, Dutch in its quiet cleanliness and dignity.

At first glance the unruliness of the garden outside might seem to challenge or dilute the pure lines of Pawson's interior. One might have thought his house would sit more perfectly at the centre of a more formal, perhaps Japanese, stonescape. In fact, it is heroically in keeping with the *mise-en-scène*, a luminous chapel amidst the greenery. The wilderness beyond his square of light, the big-limbed trees and the bustle of climbing plants, only emphasizes the coolness of Pawson's creation.

The sloping expanse of grass – not quite suburban enough to be a mere lawn – plays host in summer to picnics: it is an airy extension to the kitchen. Again, to take a picnic here, as John himself likes to do, and did often when the work was in progress, is truly to take your ease in public. When we picnic in the countryside or in a municipal park, we snatch the privacy the metropolis offers: we do not expect to see anyone we know. In the communal garden, however, we are very likely to attract sociable or inquisitive neighbours. Children flock round like gannets if they smell a sausage roll, while their parents eye up the vintage of the Pawson wine and submit that yes, well, just a small one would be lovely.

Naturally, when Pawson bought the house, his reputation had preceded him and the garden was quickly buzzing with curiosity. What would he do? Design a round house, perhaps? A lighthouse? A temple? A departure lounge? In the event the year-long project to design and renovate the house settled into the usual polite simmerings with his nearest neighbours about underpinning, hot air outlets and the ferocious squeal of the tile-cutter. But it gave us many highlights. The early weeks when what he had was a one-roomed hard-hat area full of long ladders and scaffolding (tempting to leave it that way, perhaps). The day when a pair of stonemasons from an Italian quarry sipped coffee out in the garden and discussed the precise shade of Ischian apricot that would sit well on his kitchen floor. The day when a mature cherry tree was hoisted over the roof and into the courtyard, only to burst into a flower a week or so later. Communal gardens are rare, achieving something close to a civic high point by simultaneously dividing people – pushing them apart, so that they have a hundred yards of greenery beyond their windows – and bringing them together in an enclosed space. Along with all the usual comedy of building sites went the sense that something more than a house, something more like a sculpture or a work of art, was taking shape in the bushes down there, eyes open at the back of its head.

My dogs and my youngest son like to run away along the garden path that passes John Pawson's back gate. So, long before I heard John Pawson's name, I sometimes stood peering through his weather-greyed lattice calling my truants home only half-heartedly while resting my eyes on the glass wall that shimmers like a mirage between his kitchen and his garden. I had never seen a London house which so confidently commandeered outdoor space and which was so unafraid to put its inhabitants on public view. It savoured of a warm climate, of large secluded spaces, and of nerve. The stone counter running the length of the kitchen, right through the glass wall and out to the farthest reach of the garden, seemed to say, Eat and drink where you like, as much as you like, in whatever weather.

The first few times I looked at John's house, the glass wall and the stone counter were the only two things I noticed – serene yet riveting to the eye, like a clear pool of water with a figure suspended in it. They formed a space both soothing and invigorating in which anything, it seemed, might freely happen. I felt I couldn't stare enough at those two contrasting elements, and certainly I couldn't have told you how many floors the house had or what colour it was painted. I suppose I was aware, also, of the stone paving, but only as if it were another dimension – like a fold – of the counter, extending uninterrupted from indoors to outdoors. I was a little shocked: the (then) anonymous owner of this house seemed to be getting away with a domestic idea that nobody else on the garden had – or had even thought of. And I was a little jealous.

The third thing I noticed about John's house was a pink rubber glove: wet, turned half inside out, lying on the kitchen floor beside a jam-packed rubbish bin. I saw this through the street window very early one Sunday morning as I heaved my son up the hill in his pushchair and dragged my dogs by their leads. All the neighbourhood was sleeping, and here was a messy sign of life: party debris, the washing up abandoned. In the setting, the glove looked like a piece of contemporary art, framed and intended to give the viewer pause – a human clue in a plain, geometric ground. It seemed terribly

important – a symbolic prop left behind after the actors had exited, the evidence of a crime, or perhaps the sole factual remnant of a numinous experience of some kind.

That's the thing about Pawson buildings – they set a scene so powerfully that anything placed inside them acquires an aura of being exceptionally meaningful, exceptionally valued. 'Minimalist' doesn't in my view account for the effect; on the contrary, the effect is maximal, supercharged, eerie, occasionally mystical. Yes, it is achieved through simplification – through, as John told one friend, reducing the elements in a space until nothing more can be changed. Paradoxically, this process of simplification increases visual impact. The result calls upon viewers for a special kind of attention – as when in the theatre the house lights go down, and the audience focuses away from the general glitter of life onto the small area of the lit stage.

Human beings are inventive and disorderly. In our imaginations we can pursue innumerable alternatives of form or narrative. Our paths through life, if they could be seen as line drawings, chaotically meander. When eventually I made my way inside John's house, I was stunned by how strictly the design resisted fantasy and waywardness; the steep narrow stairs were an idea of a staircase, rising as if in a dream, without evidently being attached to anything or being made from anything. Neither ornament nor technical concerns showed anywhere. Ambient light pooled here and there on surfaces, sourceless. A building is material; the house seemed cerebral – a philosophical archetype made from stone and wood that could be touched, kicked, sat on.

At first the house gave me a feeling of peaceful vitality, but what impresses me still is the sensation of energy subdued in its lines. All the possible ideas for a room, all the possible human activities which might occur in it, and all the possible possessions which might be accumulated there, are disciplined, straightened, brought to heel. The concentration, the force of mental will, to achieve this, lingers palpably in the result, and the sense of crouching power is almost frightening. I have noticed this effect in John's other buildings, too, and it is increased by his use of natural materials – mostly hard ones, stone and wood – which exude an enveloping softness through being made to succumb to the ruthlessness and completeness of the overall design.

John's sitting room, like the kitchen, conceals clutter behind tall-doored cupboards; a few chairs and a table (doubling as a sofa; John's design) stand along the raised hearth which, like the kitchen counter immediately underneath it on the floor below, single-mindedly establishes the purpose of the room, and seems to say, Gather by the fire – the Ur-use of shelter. The colours are beyond neutral; they are nonexistent. The bedrooms are merely rooms with beds and duvets; they might as well be caves or cells with animal skins thrown on the floor except they seem smoother, warmer, safer. The bath and sinks, made from rectangular slabs of limestone, might easily serve as small swimming pools or sarcophagi; they are simply containers into which water or bodies can be poured. Like everything else in the house, they obliterate fragile alternative versions in the mind's eye.

A glass ceiling above the shower slides open to the sky, so the bather can wash in the night air, or in the sun, or in the rain. When John showed it to me, I thought: In London such a shower is defiant, if not hubristic; and then, with a sensation of thrill, Why not dare? I spotted moss on the shower room floor and fleetingly pictured Ajax, sponges, damp; but practical considerations seemed trivial under the exposed wilderness of the stratosphere, and the moss took on its own beautiful significance, like the rubber glove on the kitchen floor.

To live in John's house, one would want a large spirit and a small number of possessions. John tells me he was raised entirely among grown-up older sisters whom he describes as both voluptuous and highly intelligent. His use of raw materials is opulent, but there is not a curve in his house apart from the titanically graceful chrome faucets and, in the kitchen, the extravagantly thick blown glass plates made by his sister-in-law and a super heavy tactile bronze bowl designed by himself.

Could I be comfortable in a setting where all forms of softness or colour that might be termed feminine are harshly excluded? Nowadays we so love comfort that we intricately adapt our living spaces to our physical and emotional needs until they are extensions, even expressions, of our personalities. Then, after a while, we cease to notice them, have pleasure only in showing them off to friends, and require a change of decoration to rupture the film of habit. Living in John's house would be more like having a stone in your shoe, or, if you were a princess, like having a pea under your pile of mattresses. You would always know something else was there in addition to yourself. Every day would be bracing.

I once asked John how, avowing a 'minimal' aesthetic, which implies unburdening oneself of possessions, he could design spaces to sell consumer goods. After all, the demagogic power of his architectural rhetoric makes shops look like religious sanctuaries where the purchase-yet-to-be-made appears like a grail on an altar, imbued with indefinable significance and set apart from anything that might distract the shopper from needing to get possession of it. John acknowledged the contradiction, but it didn't seem to bother him. I wondered whether he had fully shouldered the ethical responsibility that comes with successfully promulgating a doctrine; for his buildings are, in their way, doctrinaire. Contradictions are like chasms that get you right down into the deeper strata of rock, and perhaps this particular issue should be turned on its head. The religious aura surrounding a consumer item heightens awareness; it might as easily caution a shopper against thinking things can be 'acquired'. Once removed from the setting in which it is sold, once taken home and made familiar, doesn't the consumer item always lose its magic?

The first time I met him, John told me that he found it difficult to do anything in moderation. That remark now seems almost perfectly revealing. He once spent twenty-four hours exploring the possibility of becoming a monk. His buildings reveal a monastic hunger for inner life, and they embody the possibility of gratifying that hunger through the strict, even extreme, application of principles. Recently, he designed a monastery, a project which might seem to suit him better than any other, and which forced him, as building does, right up against the actual. How much should a monastery cost if a monk has taken a vow of poverty?

Before Martin Luther, spending on worship of God was run-of-the-mill, but now we all know that undertaken with the wrong attitude, such spending can only corrupt. A monk renounces worldly things in order to enrich the spirit. The monk himself does not own or have concupiscent pride in the building – at least he should not. He only uses the building, which should symbolize and perhaps remind him of the home he longs to go to in heaven: simple in the fact that it is perfect, mysterious in the fact that he can't fully understand it… yet. If it cost a great deal to build a monastery or if it cost little, the building ought to be an 'offering' to God or it ought to embody the difficulty and the beauty of the way of life that is devoted to trying to understand God's will. Perhaps ideally it would be and do both.

John's house creates a quasi-religious atmosphere for domestic activities and relationships. When I say quasi, I don't mean fake, because the house evokes an authentic sense of awe. The family is perhaps our most ubiquitous and turbulent institution – whether we mean mother/father/child or some other long-term bond that engenders a home – and domestic routine is a central archetype of human action. Why not bring to our ordinary daily rituals our most sacramental attitude? We need not renounce the world, as monks do, but John's house seems to suggest that we might, in a more focused setting, achieve a richer experience of our necessary and familiar private pursuits. This is a large ambition though certainly a worthy one. Domestic life is a mystery; in it we minister to those we have chosen or created; in it we try to plumb the depths of the thing we call love.

The Japanese have a word 'wabi' to denote 'poverty', or rather, 'voluntary poverty' – in the Zen sense that to be 'thingless' is to possess the world. In both China and Japan, this ascetic search for 'poverty' derives from the teaching of the Buddha. A man weighted down by things, he said, was like a ship into which water is pouring: the only hope of reaching safety was to jettison the cargo.

'Man', in the words of a great Zen master, 'originally possesses nothing'. Yet the idea that a 'poor art' is both more liberating and enduring than 'rich art' has been the mainspring, paradoxically, behind many of the most treasured masterpieces of the Far East. A trained eye can tell at a glance which tea-ceremony bowl genuinely possesses the spirit of 'wabi', and which does not.

'Poor art', however – mute, featureless, an-iconic – is not, and never has been, confined to the East alone. In the Old Testament you can read of Jehovah's fury to find that His Children had polluted the Temple, by cramming its courts with images, and so turning it into a sculpture gallery. If the Lord had to settle anywhere, he must at least be able to breathe, in His sanctuary, a little of the pure air of Sinai.

To strip down, to purify, to breathe again, to remove the scum and the gilding – has been a constant theme of Judaeo-Christianity, and so of the Western tradition. For examples of 'wabi' in the West, one must look to certain Cistercian abbeys, to the 'empty' churches of Sanraedam, the buildings of the Shakers, the piano music of Satie, or Cézanne's final watercolours of Mont Saint-Victoire. Towards the end of his life, Mark Rothko said he hoped his paintings would resemble the 'sides of a tent'. This is not, of course, to say that 'poverty' of this kind is exclusive to great artists: it could also be present in an ordinary Nonconformist chapel.

What is not generally recognized is that 'emptiness' in architecture – or empty space – is not empty, but full: yet to realise this fullness requires the most exacting standards and discipline from the architect. Here, there can be no room for uncertainty or anxious 'artistic' effects. Either the work must be perfect, or not at all. Architecture is 'frozen music': the more you reduce, the more perfect its notes must be. I once went to see a former pupil of Mies van der Rohe, who had put into effect the master's dictum, 'Less is more'. He lived in a spare one-room apartment in mid-town Manhattan. He was a very rich man. All his possessions he kept in cupboards – and among them was a cubist Picasso. I recall him saying that if you had to live in a crass, claustrophobic twentieth-century city; if, outside your door, you were bombarded by the demands of consumerism – 'BUY ME! OBEY ME! – the greatest of all luxuries was to be able to walk, unimpeded by furniture or pictures, around your own bare walls. For, no matter how small the room, providing your eye could travel freely around it, the space it contained was limitless. He was repeating, in effect, the premise underlying medieval monasticism that the monk who sat in his cell was free to travel everywhere.

About five years ago, without the least forewarning of what to expect, I was taken to a flat in an ornate but slightly down-at-heel Victorian terrace, and shown into a room in which, it seemed to me, the notes were almost perfect.

It was the first realised work of John Pawson; yet the product of fifteen years hard thinking as to how such a room could be. Here, at last, I felt, was someone who understood that a room – any room, anywhere – should be a space in which to dream. It was the real thing: a room with 'wabi'. I walked around the walls, watching its planes, shadows and proportions in a state of near-elation.

Pawson comes from a line of hard-working Yorkshire mill-owners. He was sent to Eton with a Yorkshire accent, and insisted on sleeping in a white canvas hammock. At the age of 25, after seven years in the family business, he left England for Japan, where he taught at a University in Nagoya. He trained his eye on Japanese buildings, from the most venerated temples to the simplest peasant house. To his friendship with the architect, Shiro Kuramata, he owes the insight that you can make the most daring experiments with new materials and new technology without having to sacrifice the spirit of 'poverty'.

To live in one of his interiors is not for the lazy or lazy-minded; it requires a certain act of will. What it does not

require is a hair-shirted mentality.
This kind of 'reduction' is not the
antithesis of enjoyment, but invigorating
and enjoyable. Any 'thing' retained is
forever pressed into proving its worth.
Any useless 'thing' chucked out is a gain.

The construction of the monastery at Novy Dvur aims first and foremost to provide the young Czech monks who started their studies at Sept-Fons a place to continue their monastic way of life. If the nature of this project dictated that we choose an architect attuned to the monastic spirit, then the choice of Mr Pawson clashed with certain longstanding preconceived ideas – that contemporary art is pretentious and expensive, that beauty is always associated with the idea of luxury and so on. (It should be noted that the churches and monasteries built over the last 150 years which have adhered to this way of thinking have not themselves all been successes.)

When the abbot of Sept-Fons and a brother, both conversant with contemporary architecture, left for London, the monks expressed reservation. In the end, the legacy of our tradition which privileges architecture and the care with which we approach every detail, came down on the side of daring. What we all agreed upon was the quality of Mr Pawson's work, all the more because of his understanding of the Cistercian aesthetic.

The project moved rapidly and seduced us all. We were unanimous in our decision to house the church in the grange at Novy Dvur. Mr Pawson grasped immediately that we needed a church whose raison d'être could not be misunderstood, either by us or our visitors. We appreciated his prescience. He felt, as we did, that a couple of months would be sufficient to complete the plans. No more than he could we imagine how long it would actually take to plan – in every detail – the construction of spaces which support the life of a community. The process of detailing is, as I write, ongoing. The clash between his design and our requirements has occasionally led to conflict, but a conflict which is never terminal. Through this we have gained a better understanding of the nature of the space in which we live, of the constraints of simplicity and poverty and of the two temptations – each equally pernicious – of ostentation and mediocrity. In this line of questioning, we monks have always played our part.

Mr Pawson hopes that the monastery of Our Lady at Novy Dvur will be perfect. If he will forgive us, we are convinced that this is impossible. The chapels at Ronchamp and Vence, the convent at La Tourette, these modern masterpieces, along with the churches of Audincourt or of Assy, are not perfect. Are they museums, or places of worship and community life? Architectural glory is not the cause of all the difficulties they have faced in their short histories; on the other hand who can say what part it has played? Success is, however, possible – the monastery at Vals, built by the talented Father van der Laan, still shelters a thriving community.

We are in agreement with Mr Pawson in saying that architecture has an impact on the soul. Just as sacred music reaches its zenith when it gives place of prominence to the text it supports, so the cloister and church at Novy Dvur will probably have the sublime perfection of architecture which effaces itself in the service of religious spirit. In building for the monks, Mr Pawson, absolute Minimalist that he already is, has had to develop an even more radical approach to simplicity. Occasionally we have had to restrict him, sometimes strongly, often for economic reasons. But even if the architect sometimes resisted, the man understood both what we expected of him and the characteristic we most admire in him – namely that he knows how to listen to us without ceasing to defend his own preferences.

The monastery at Novy Dvur, even before it is finished, represents perhaps the most significant religious and architectural event in Central Europe of this century. It will be lived in by contemplatives separated from the world by their vocation. In ten, fifty or a hundred years, if the monks are strong in their faith – and with the grace of God – the community and architecture will be fused as one. While waiting for that eventuality, let us pay tribute to the man and to the architect, for this work that can only ever be partially open to the regard of others, just like the life of a monk, essentially hidden from the world.

071
The noise and dust of the city
are filtered out.

Calvin Klein first approached Pawson to create a flagship store for him in New York. Completed in 1995, Pawson's reinvention of a handsome neoclassical building on Madison Avenue quickly achieved the status of landmark architecture.

Pawson's approach was to treat store design as being, in essence, no different from any other type of design. The key was spatial quality – if the space was good, the clothes would look good and the customer feel good. Working with a limited palette of materials, Pawson created interiors characterized by an unusual clarity of line and surface – rare anywhere, but virtually unprecedented in a store. This was architecture which was the product of an accumulation of perfectly executed details. Pawson demonstrated that an uncompromising aesthetic could be entirely consistent with an immaculately functioning retail environment.

The continuities between the architecture of Pawson's design for the new Paris store on Avenue Montaigne and his earlier work for Klein are clear. In New York, the challenge was to insert new accommodation in a way which did not disrupt the handsome proportions of the original interior. In Paris pressure on floor space prevents the incorporation of extensive double-height elements, but Pawson has created spare, sensual white spaces where proportion and light are perfect – a pristine showcase for the collections and the latest in a series of subtle redefinitions of modern luxury for Klein.

Calvin Klein Store, Paris

072
The interior unfolds as a
sequence of immaculate,
uninterrupted surfaces.

073, 074
Recesses in the walls act as
light boxes.

075
Calvin Klein Store,
Madison Avenue,
New York, 1995

Calvin Klein Store, Paris

076, 077, 078, 079
The store seduces and supplies
with equal discretion.

079

080
The design is configured so that the production wing enjoys the most dramatic outlook, tempting workers engaged in painstaking close work to rest their eyes on views which stretch from the canal and trees of the site to a skyline of mountains.

A key challenge of this design for a new headquarters and factory for the long-established firm of Swiss watchmakers, Vacheron Constantin, was to harmonize architecture of the highest aesthetic quality with a very particular set of technical requirements.

The design consists of five vast honey-coloured concrete mantles set in a formal landscape. Working on a monumental scale and without an unnecessary or superfluous gesture, Pawson uses a series of pristine junctions to explore the very different qualities of stone and glass, playing with the ability of glass to make stone appear to float.

By using structures which are supported at their ends and by columns, Pawson is able to run uninterrupted clerestories along the lengths of all interior spaces, creating a frieze of natural light which becomes a defining characteristic of the architecture. Light also filters in from above, through a repeating grid of skylights. Two internal courtyards – one open to the sky, each framed in glass – increase light and transparency in the heart of the architecture. Vistas slicing through the architecture – both along the main lines of the grid and diagonally – give views out into the landscape and glimpses of people working in other parts of the complex.

One of Pawson's intentions here is to counter the feeling of isolation which is usual in large workplaces, balancing the need for privacy with the human desire for a socialized environment.

081

082

081
The architecture is positioned for
maximum visibility from the road.

082, 083
Rhythmic repetition of the
interior elements reinforces the
sense of order and calm.

083

Vacheron Constantin, Geneva

084
Views out become part of the
landscape of the interior.

085
The combination of natural and
ambient light produces interiors
characterized by their luminosity.

086
Etched glass screens divide the
working spaces.

087
A grid of skylights allows
natural light into the core of
the architecture.

Pawson's design for the redevelopment of a striking urban riverside site in the north of England has to house a broad range of functions, including the town's market and museum. Rather than assign separate territories to each, Pawson superimposes the two functions within one double-height, light-filled space. The grid of market stalls and the grid of museum display cases are overlaid upon one another, with all elements designed so that the space reads coherently. The solution has the merit of economic logic, but is also curatorially innovative. In place of architecture which formalizes the distinctions between functions, Pawson has created a model which fosters resonances between ostensibly diverse activities.

One of the goals of the Radcliffe project is to make art part of the everyday life of people who might not be in the habit of visiting a gallery. On the lower floor, a central gallery surrounded by broad, cloister-like passages is dedicated to a permanent exhibition of work by the sculptor Ulrich Ruckriem. A rill diverted from the river runs through the gallery. This rill is the most visible evidence of the importance Pawson gives to the relationship between the new architecture and its riverside setting. Light playing on the surface of the water reflects on to smooth stone and plaster planes, adding to the contemplative quality of these spare interiors.

088

089

088
A restaurant is one of many elements to be fitted within the skin of the new architecture.

089
Market and museum occupy a single, double-height space.

090
The scheme redefines the relationship of the site with its river setting.

091, 092
The Ruckriem Gallery comprises
a main gallery surrounded by
broad, cloister-like passages,
with pieces installed throughout.
Lines of light cast up on the
ceiling frame the central space.

093
Along the wall bordering the
river a narrow rill diverts water
through the gallery.

094
The cantilevered master bedroom
is part of the interlocking of
architecture and landscape
evident throughout the house.

Strategies for building on a sloped site fall into two main categories. On the one hand an architect may choose to cancel out the effect of the slope – through the construction of a podium, through excavation, or by setting a structure on stilts. Pawson's design for a private house in Germany adopts the other, gentler strategy, following the slope and making it a defining part of the character of the architecture.

Pawson's design presents a single storey to the street, but steps down to accommodate a second storey on the garden side. Entrance to the main living areas on the lower level is down a double flight of stairs, with sunlight filtering in from a skylight running the length of the stairwell. Private family quarters are upstairs, parents and children occupying their own wings, connected by a spa room.

Nature shapes more than the contours of this house. Extensive glazed panels on the garden side frame woodland views which become part of the landscape of the interior, while a glass cantilevered section in the main bedroom gives a sense of being out amongst the treetops.

Of particular interest here is the way in which Pawson has created architecture which dissolves the conventional barriers between inside and outside, but not at the price of intimate interior spaces. Instead, in his hands, landscape becomes an essential part of the domestic cocoon.

Private House, Germany

095, 097
The architecture fits itself to the
shape of the land.

096
A restricted palette of natural
materials – predominantly stone
and timber – is used inside
and out.

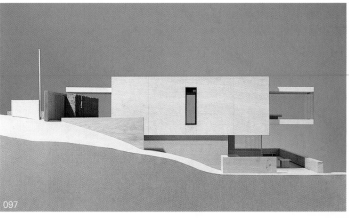

Private House, Germany

Each part of the house has its
own distinct characters – open
or closed, public or private.

098
Living room

099
Spa room

100
Entrance

101
Kitchen

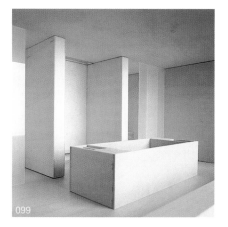

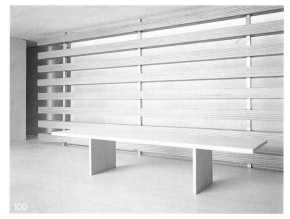

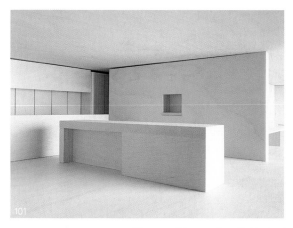

102
Natural light emphasizes the
drama of the stairwell.

Pawson used his own family house as an opportunity to explore exhaustively how domestic architecture can be designed around the key rituals – eating, sleeping, bathing – which will take place within it. The result is a house in which everything has been considered, reduced, simplified, but one where, crucially, the process of paring down has uncovered, rather than removed, meaning.

The raw material was a traditional mid-nineteenth-century row house without the row in west London. It is an example of a type found all over London, in this instance made extraordinary by unimpeded views of communal gardens to both the front and the back.

Pawson stripped out the old interior in its entirety, clearing away the dog-leg staircases and attendant L-shaped floor plans. A single straight flight of stairs now rises from the ground to the top of the house, with a second flight underneath to the basement. The new arrangement creates a five metre band of uninterrupted space on every floor.

While planning regulations prohibited alterations to the facade, the rear elevation has been sliced open, with a glass wall at basement level and an enlarged aperture on the first floor. At the top of the house a glazed slot running the length of the ceiling allows daylight to spill down through the triple-height stairwell, whilst the glass ceiling of the sky shower slides away to permit bathing under the sun or stars. In places the threshold between inside and out is minimized to the point that it all but disappears.

103

104

105

106

Pawson House, London

103
The old interior was scooped out, leaving the skin intact.

104, 108, 109
The stone worktop runs from the front of the house, extending the length of the garden and formalizing the fusion of interior and exterior spaces as a single room, part of whose ceiling is the sky.

105, 106
The ground floor is entirely reinvented as contemporary living space.

107
The house lies within a conservation area, with restrictions on alterations to the front. The traditional facade gives only a tantalizing hint of the new life which has been flipped into the frame of the old.

110

111

110
The entrance is dominated by
the underside of the main flight
of stairs which rises the full
height of the house.

111, 112
This is architecture which
celebrates the rituals of daily life.
Clarity of space, line and surface
is sanctified by clarity of function.

113
The stairs are the key to the
new design.

114
The church affords the most
powerful expression of
Pawson's treatment of light in
the new monastery. At certain
times of day, a combination of
direct and diffused light will give
the altar the appearance of
floating in a haze of
luminescence.

Authentically simple environments are inevitably
the outcome of complex architectural processes.
Nowhere, perhaps, is this more true than within the
enclosed world of the cloister. Seamlessness is here
more than an aesthetic preference. An absence of
visual distraction supports the goal of monastic life,
which is concentration on the deity. A monastery's
function should be as smooth and flawless as its
volumes and surfaces.

The Cistercian movement has always placed great
emphasis on the relationship between theology and
architecture. The commission to design a new
foundation for the order in Bohemia offered Pawson
a rare opportunity to re-examine this relationship.
The commission has required Pawson to refine his
vocabulary, in order that he might express the Cistercian
spirit with absolute precision, in a language free of
pastiche, but charged with poetry.

The finished monastery of Novy Dvur will sit in 100
hectares of remote farmland, surrounded by wooded
hills. One of the key challenges of the project was to
decide what elements of the pre-existing architecture
should be kept and, following from this, the relationship
between new and original architecture.

Pawson's scheme retains the baroque manor house
and courtyard configuration, but clears away the
remains of dilapidated barns, allowing the church and
three sides of the cloister to consist of entirely new
architecture. The design envisages an harmonious
marriage of new and old, with no unnecessary drama
at the junctions. In keeping with Cistercian aesthetic
preoccupations, Pawson has created an architecture
of light, dramatic effects of light being perfectly
consistent with an atmosphere of serenity.

115

116

117

115, 116
At the time of acquisition, the
site had lain uninhabited for
more than forty years. As one of
the monks said on an early visit,
'Even in ruins, it is very beautiful.
It has soul; it is true.'

117
The baroque manor house was
the work of Dientzenhofer,
architect of Prague's St Nicolas
church and Brevnov monastery.
Following extensive historical
research and measured surveys,
a process of painstaking
restoration has been undertaken.

118
The cloister is the heart of the
monastic city, giving access to
all the major spaces within the
community – church, sacristy,
chapter house, infirmary,
scriptorium, chapels, refectory
and library.

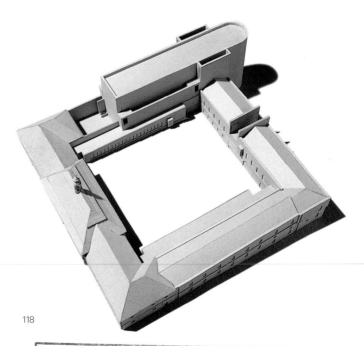

118

119
The cantilevered construction of the cloister at Novy Dvur has no precedent in monastic architecture. Aside from the purity of the volumes it creates, the design allows for glazing to run uninterrupted the length of each wing – discreet but essential protection from the harsh Bohemian winters. Pools of water cast reflections upward, dappling the white vaulted ceilings.

120
The monastery is set on a slope, with the line of building following the gradient.

121
The church will be used by local people and by vistors, although access for these outsiders will be separate from that used by the monks. A guest house forms part of the scheme.

122
The quality of the luminous interior of the chapter house will be most striking when glimpsed from the brighter environment of the cloister.

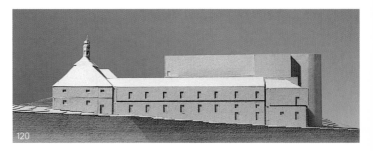

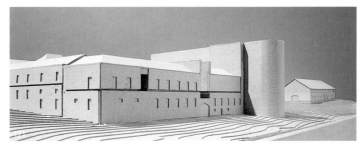

John Pawson's studio occupies two floors – ground and basement – behind Kings Cross station, facing the vast building site which will one day be London's new Eurostar terminal. Taxis and buses grind past. Pedestrians kick the windows, occasionally stooping to peer down into a strange subterranean world, at faces lit by the unearthly light cast from computer screens, pink neon from the Dan Flavin installation seeping across white plaster walls and poured concrete floors.

The serene volumes of the double-height studio have been carved out of what was formerly industrial space. Light and shadow play on white planes. A signature vertiginous flight of stairs with no rail connects the two floors. There is an abstract, almost spiritual quality to the place.

At the back, screened by the stairwell there is a large, eclectic library. Additional shelved stacks house an exhaustive archive. Virtually every sequence in this vast array of identical black files represents physical space somewhere in the world outside – places which once only existed in the architect's head.

At any one time around a dozen people are busy at the long worktables. Although nothing is private in this open-plan environment, people are instinctively territorial – hot-desking is reserved for collaborators who spend time here, but who are not resident. There is little in the way of conventional hierarchy. We work in close proximity to one another and the sense of belonging to a team is strong. This is a group of people which shares more than working space – it shares a vision of what the perfect space might be like and is collectively engaged in its realization.

A common vision is not the same thing as constant harmony. Exchanges can be animated, silences menacing and once or twice things have been thrown. Sometimes it feels that lofty though the space we inhabit is, still it threatens to afford insufficient volume for the personalities it contains.

People perhaps assume that in an age of advanced technology, architecture and design may be practised in spaces of monastic calm and emptiness – the artist and his screen. The reality is still a myriad of materials and tools – books, paper, pens, scalpels, rulers, glue, foam board, plans and sketches pinned to walls, models made up to various scales.

The office as it is constantly pitches itself against a pristine vision of how it should be. It is not the sporadically chaotic reality that is unusual, it is the absoluteness of the ideal. The practice offers to others a utopian vision of space in which there is a place for everything and everything in its place. That it is not itself quite such a place consistently is inevitable, but distressing. As a result, it is a place of sudden purges, when the instinct to horde is consumed by the more powerful instinct to clear – as Bruce Chatwin puts it, 'to strip down, to purify, to breathe again'.

At this interface between order and its opposite, in a slow and rigorous process, proportions are perfected, surfaces smoothed and junctions minimized, advancing a body of work which started long before John's first commercial commission, when, at the age of sixteen and still living at home, he decided to simplify an inglenook fireplace, replacing it with a plain cantilevered slate slab.

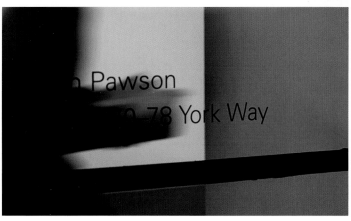

The abbey of Le Thoronet in Provence, a highpoint of twelfth-century Cistercian architecture, has fascinated and inspired many architects – notably Le Corbusier, who famously contributed a preface to *Architecture of Truth*, Lucien Hervé's book of photographs documenting the abbey, first published in the 1950s. For John Pawson Le Thoronet has been a subject of continuing interest – a sublime example of architecture rooted in faith and a moving sense of simplicity. Pawson was responsible for the design of the new edition of Hervé's book, published in 2001. Christoph Kicherer's new photographs eloquently reflect the abbey's enduring significance.

van Royen Apartment,
Hester van Royen,
London, 1981

Chatwin Apartment,
Bruce Chatwin,
London, 1982

Audi Apartment,
Pierre Audi,
London, 1984

Waddington Apartment,
Ferriel Waddington,
London, 1985

van Royen Apartment,
Hester van Royen,
London, 1986

Abu Saad Apartment,
Lelia and Walid Abu Saad,
London, 1986

Waddington House,
Clodagh and Leslie Waddington,
London, 1986

Neuendorf Apartment,
Carolina and Hans Neuendorf,
Frankfurt, 1987

Saatchi House,
Doris Saatchi,
London, 1987

Bock Apartment,
Vivienne Bock,
London, 1987

Miro House,
Victoria and Warren Miro,
London, 1988

Craig-Martin Studio,
Michael Craig-Martin,
London, 1988

Neuendorf House,
Carolina and Hans Neuendorf,
Majorca, 1989

Rothman Apartment,
Florence and Noel Rothman,
London, 1990

van Royen Apartment,
Hester van Royen,
London, 1991

Audi House,
Pierre Audi,
Amsterdam, 1993

Donnelly House,
Marie and Joe Donnelly,
Dublin, 1993

Tarn House,
Gary Tarn,
London, 1993

Pawson House,
Catherine and John Pawson,
London, 1994

Tilty Barn,
Fi McGhee and Sean Perkins,
Essex, 1995

van Moerkerke House,
Sophie van Moerkerke,
London, 1996

Palmano House,
Cindy Palmano,
London, 1996

Zander House,
David Zander,
Los Angeles, 1996 (unbuilt)

Donnelly House,
Marie and Joe Donnelly,
Dublin, 1996 (unbuilt)

Mas des Pradelles,
Janet and Gilbert de Botton,
Provence, 1998

Lagerfeld Apartment,
Karl Lagerfeld,
Paris, 1998 (unbuilt)

Guesthouse and Pool,
Karl Lagerfeld,
Biarritz, 1998 (unbuilt)

Evins Apartment,
Melissa Evins,
New York, 1999

Faggionato Apartment,
Anne Faggionato and Mungo Park,
London, 1999

Pawson House,
Catherine and John Pawson,
London, 1999

Glynn House,
Lisa and Richard Glynn,
London, 1999

Hauptman House,
Ellen and Andrew Bronfman Hauptman,
London, 1999

Booth Garden,
Lauren and Mark Booth,
London, 2000

The Pond House,
Martha Stewart,
Long Island, 2000 (unbuilt)

Millennium Tower,
James Harvey,
London, 2000 (unbuilt)

Pember Road Development,
Anthony MacLlwaine,
London, 2000 (unbuilt)

Telluride House,
Catherine Walsh,
Colorado, 2001

Blakstad House,
Lucy Blakstad and Adrian Caddy,
London, 2001

Wilheim House,
John Wilheim,
California, 2001

Wardour Castle,
Nigel Tuersley,
Wiltshire, 2001

Starkmann House,
Bernard and Marie Starkmann,
Seychelles, 2002

Yuki House,
Yuki,
London, 2002

Novy Dvur Monastery,
Abbaye Notre-Dame de Sept-Fons,
Czech Republic, 2002/3

Private House,
Germany, 2003

Lansdowne Lodge Apartments,
Grainger Trust,
London, 2003

Taira House,
Tatsuo Taira,
Okinawa, 2003

Private Villa,
Qatar, 2003

Delafontaine House,
Beatrice Delafontaine,
Knokke, 2003

Calvin Klein Apartment,
Calvin Klein,
New York, 2003

Commercial

JCB Visitors Centre,
JCB,
Rocester, 1986 (unbuilt)

Wakaba Restaurant,
Kieko and Minoru Yoshihara,
London, 1987

Starkmann Offices,
Starkmann Library Services,
London, 1988

Cannelle Cake Shop,
Raja Cortas,
London, 1988

RK RK Shop,
Rajindra Dhawan,
London, 1988

Wagamama Restaurant,
Alan Yau,
London, 1991

Calvin Klein Store,
Calvin Klein Inc,
Tokyo, 1994

Jurgen Lehl Store,
Jurgen Lehl Co,
Kumamoto, 1995

GAM Conference Suite,
Gilbert de Botton,
London, 1995

Calvin Klein Store,
Calvin Klein Inc,
New York, 1995

Sun Assurance Building,
Bernard van Moerkerke,
Ostend, 1995 (unbuilt)

Calvin Klein Store,
Calvin Klein Inc,
Seoul, 1996

Jigsaw Store,
Robinson Webster Holdings Ltd,
London, 1996

Jigsaw Store,
Marui Trading Japan,
Yokohama, 1996

Jigsaw Store,
Marui Trading Japan,
Shizuoka, 1996

Obumex Kitchen System,
Obumex,
Belgium, 1996

York Way Offices,
John Pawson,
London 1997

The Young Vic Theatre,
Young Vic Theatre,
London, 1997 (unbuilt)

Cathay Pacific Lounges,
Cathay Pacific,
Hong Kong, 1998

7L Bookshop and Studio,
Karl Lagerfeld,
Paris, 1998 (unbuilt)

El Horria Studio,
Karl Lagerfeld,
Biarritz, 1998 (unbuilt)

Calvin Klein Men's Store,
Calvin Klein Inc,
Paris, 1998

CK Jeanswear,
Calvin Klein Inc,
Bluewater, 1999

CK Jeanswear,
Calvin Klein Inc,
Hamburg, 1999

CK Jeanswear,
Calvin Klein Inc,
Dubai, 1999

Calvin Klein Store,
Calvin Klein Inc,
Fukuoka, 1999

Calvin Klein Store,
Calvin Klein Inc,
Taipei, 2000

Bulthaup Showroom,
The Kitchen People,
London, 2000

250 Brompton Road,
Chelsfield Plc,
London, 2001

Door Handle Collection,
Valli & Valli,
London, 2001

Furniture Collection,
Driade,
Italy, 2001

5 Items,
When Objects Work,
Belgium, 2001

Batavia Building,
Sodium,
Amsterdam, 2001 (unbuilt)

Cookware Collection,
Demeyere,
Belgium, 2002

Sabbe Offices,
Jean Louis Sabbe,
Blankenberge, 2002

Calvin Klein Collection Store,
Calvin Klein Inc,
Paris, 2002

Skysuite Offices,
Chelsfield Plc,
London, 2002

John Pawson Collection 2,
When Objects Work,
Belgium, 2002

Marketmuseum,
Bury Metropolitan Council,
Radcliffe, 2004

Galleries and Exhibitions

Waddington Galleries,
Clodagh and Leslie Waddington,
London, 1983

Boilerhouse Exhibition,
Victoria and Albert Museum,
London, 1984

Objects Exhibition,
Environment,
London, 1986

PPOW Gallery,
Penny Wilkington and Wendy Olsdorf,
New York, 1986

Runkel Hue-Williams Gallery,
Michael Hue-Williams and
Claus Runkel,
London, 1988

Neuendorf Art Centre,
Carolina and Hans Neuendorf,
Germany, 1989 (unbuilt)

Fusion Gallery,
Dominic Berning,
London, 1990

Connaught Brown Gallery,
Anthony Brown,
London, 1990

The Raw and the Cooked,
Museum of Modern Art,
Oxford, 1994

Michael Hue-Williams Gallery,
Michael Hue-Williams,
London, 1996

GOMA Exhibition,
UK City of Architecture,
Glasgow, 1996

Martin Smith Exhibition,
Boijmans Museum,
Rotterdam, 1996

New Times, New Thinking Exhibition,
Crafts Council,
London, 1996

Lucy Rie and Hans Coper,
Barbican Art Centre,
London, 1997

John Pawson,
IVAM,
Valencia, 2002

Architecture Biennale,
Venice, 2002

Books

John Pawson,
Gustavo Gilli, 1992

Critic,
Daishinsha Inc, 1995

Minimum,
Phaidon Press, 1996

Kitchen,
Obumex, 1998

John Pawson,
Gustavo Gilli, 1998

Mini Minimum,
Phaidon Press, 1998

Brompton Road,
Chelsfield Plc, 1999

Barn,
Booth-Clibborn Editions, 1999

John Pawson Works,
Deyan Sudjic,
Phaidon Press, 2000

Architecture of Truth,
Lucien Hervé,
Phaidon Press, 2000

Living and Eating,
John Pawson and Annie Bell,
Ebury Press, 2001